G000130930

Text by Lois Rock
Illustrations copyright © 2004 Anna C. Leplar
This edition copyright © 2004 Lion Publishing

The moral rights of the author and illustrator
have been asserted

Published by
Lion Publishing plc
Mayfield House, 256 Banbury Road,
Oxford OX2 7DH, England
www.lion-publishing.co.uk
ISBN 0 7459 4627 5

First edition 2004
1 3 5 7 9 10 8 6 4 2 0

A catalogue record for this book is available
from the British Library

Typeset in 15/19 Elegant Garamond BT
Printed and bound in Singapore

all about God

Lois Rock

Illustrated by Anna C. Leplar

LION
Children's Books

You often hear people talking about God, but you never see God!

So who is God? It's quite a mystery!

Before the beginning, Christians believe, there was God – only God.

No one made God, because God always was, and God always will be.

God is the One Who Is.

There is one everlasting God.

Long ago the everlasting God spoke: 'Let there be light.'

And there was light.

Then God made the sky and everything in it. God made the earth and everything on it.

God made the world.

God set the world spinning round the golden sun. God brought summer and winter, the time for seeds to grow and the time for crops to ripen.

God takes care of the world.

God made people –
to love God,
to love one another
and to take care of the world.

God loves people.

God chose some people to be messengers, telling others how to live as God wants. God wants people
to be fair and honest in all they do,
to take care of those in need,
to mend quarrels
and to live as friends together.

God helps people
decide what to do.

But people make mistakes. People get things wrong.
So God sent Jesus to tell people about God's forgiveness.

'God is like a good shepherd,' said Jesus, 'who searches for a sheep that has got lost and brings it safely home.'

God forgives people.

People who want to feel at home with God can talk to God in prayer.

Some prayers are thank-you prayers.

Some prayers are sorry prayers.

Some prayers are asking prayers.

God listens to prayers.

In their prayers people can ask God to help them live in the way that is good and right. They believe God will make them strong inside.

God helps people to do what is right.

In their prayers people can tell God about the things that make them happy and the things that make them sad. They believe God is close to them in good times and sad times.

God comforts people.

The people who love God believe they can trust God, even if something happens that is scary and dangerous. They believe God is watching over them with love.

God looks after people.

Everything that is alive in this world is only here for a little time. Things live and they grow, but one day they will die.

God can never die, and everything God made is safe in God's love.

God's love is the strongest thing of all.

People who love God say that when this world grows old and comes to an end, there will always be God.

They call the place where God is heaven, and those whom God loves will be safe with God in heaven for ever.

In heaven people will see God.